MW01065968

WHAT IS THE MEANING OF LIFE?

WHAT <u>IS</u>
THE
MEANING
<u>OF</u> LIFE?*

{ *AND 92 OTHER THINGS I
DON'T HAVE ANSWERS TO }

DON HERMANN

Andrews McMeel
PUBLISHING®

So, what *is* the meaning of life?

That, you know, I can't answer.

But I'm eighty-three years old, and I have lived life. I have had ample time to ponder life's not-so-little mysteries.

When I think back to the questions I asked myself when I was twenty, they're surprisingly similar to the questions I asked myself when I was forty. And sixty. Such as: Were the fears in my life pushing me to engage in things or frightening me away? And now as an octogenarian, I still haven't answered that question. You know what else I've wondered: Am I a different person behind the wheel of my car? Does it give me license to be a jerk? I also think about whether I have learned to forgive and have found things in my life that make me feel really good.

We all have our own wonders, and now in my eighties, much of what I've learned is that I don't have answers to many of these questions. But I keep asking questions, some that are philosophical, some that are outlandish, and some that are just plain silly.

For me, collecting them in one place here in this book has allowed me to think about all the experiences, the good and bad times, and to figure out what I've really learned. What I've learned is that I need to keep asking questions.

So be honest with yourself when you read this, as you may be surprised by what you learn. I hope it will be introspective, self-deprecating, insightful, and fun. After all, these questions are really about *you*.

What is the meaning of life?

Would you let a priest babysit your kids?

Do you set the bar
higher for others than you
do for yourself?

Are you quick to forgive
your adversaries but not your
loved ones?

Does fear frighten or
motivate you?

Is "I told you so"
in your arsenal?

What is the worst thing
you have to do on a
regular basis?

Are you a different person
behind the wheel of a car?

Does referring to someone as African-American, Hispanic-American, or Italian-American unite or divide us?

Do you dress to please
yourself or others?

Do you treat men and
women differently?

Do you take pleasure in
another's failure?

Why do we remember
the TV commercials but
not the products?

Do you find it difficult to say
"I was wrong"?

Would you like to be
more spontaneous?

Are you comfortable eating
alone in a restaurant?

Do celebrities influence
your choices?

Why does your voicemail
message sound so unlike you?

Is there someone
you know whom you would
really like to punch?

What's your most
embarrassing accident?

Who is on your enemies list?

Have you made your
parents proud?

Is there someone up there
laughing at us?

Can the world sustain
another world war?

Whose flaws remind you
of your own?

What's your craziest
superstition?

Do you go with your gut?

What's your most regrettable
"missed opportunity"?

Do you forgive and forget?

What is the gutsiest thing
you've ever done?

Are you afraid to fail?

Why does violence draw
us like a magnet?

Why do we repeat the
same mistakes?

Is peace what we really want?

Do you embellish
your accomplishments?

Does it all come down
to money?

What would you change
about your body?

How many people know
"the real you"?

Do you worry about
fitting in?

Do you judge people by the way they shake hands?

Why would you like to have
you as a friend?

Does guilt get in your way?

Do you take yourself
too seriously?

Why isn't there a term limit for members of congress, senators, and judges?

Can you count the people you really trust on one hand?

Who in your life has the most contagious laugh?

Is it easier to say
"no" than "yes"?

Should the United States have mandatory government service?

Should you spank your kids?

What would you change about the election process?

Have you ever marched
for a cause?

Do you struggle with change?

What makes relationships
so much work?

Are politicians more loyal
to their parties or
to their consciences?

What makes you feel
really good?

Can you think of a
politician you would buy a
used car from?

How often do you
feel lonely?

How accurate are your
first impressions?

What would you do
if your child were
being bullied at school?

How important is it
for you to win?

How do you soothe
your anger?

Do you give
thoughtful gifts?

When was the last time
you donated to charity?

Are you good-looking?

Do your friends think
you're smart?

What's the biggest lie
you've told?

Should college athletes
be paid?

What's the worst thing
someone could say about you?

What are you fooling
yourself about?

Who has taught you the best
lesson you've ever learned?

How has a role model
disappointed you?

What happens when
you die?

What's the biggest secret
you've blabbed?

What's your worst bad habit?

What's *one* thing
you'd do differently in
raising *your* kids?

Would you donate a
kidney to a friend?

What's the one piece
of technology you can't
live without?

How many people call you
their "best friend"?

What was the one
event that most changed
your course in life?

How do you
respond to criticism?

Can you make
someone laugh?

What's worth suffering for?

Has all the hard work
really paid off?

What don't you want others
to know about you?

What's been your life's
toughest compromise?

Do you resist going
to the doctor?

Have you caught the
breaks you think you deserve?

What one act in your life has
most affected another?

Are you *really* with your
soul mate?

What's a moral issue you've
switched sides on?

What age would you
really like to be?

Would you go into a burning
house to save your pet?

What was the most difficult
day of your life?

Don brings more than forty years of award-winning advertising and marketing experience to authoring his first book at eighty-three.

After cutting his teeth in the ad world creating and producing KFC's first national advertising campaign commemorating the Colonel's seventy-fifth birthday—the ad became the largest-pulling ad in *Look* magazine's history—Don's first full-time job was with super-creative agency DKG in the late '60s, where he served as Group Head.

He then went on to create his own agency, Don Hermann & the Cream of the Crop, before joining forces with industry powerhouses to create Kolker, Talley, Hermann, where he served as President.

His leadership at KTH spawned innovative campaigns for *Ms. Magazine*, Ferrara Foods ("Holy Cannoli" campaign with Phil Rizzuto),

The New York Yankees ("Watch The Legend Grow" featuring PA announcer Bob Sheppard), and the Effie-award–winning Louis Roederer Champagne campaign. This led to a Phil Dougherty feature in *The New York Times*.

In semiretirement, Don went on to create Unbeatables, a multicultural education firm that included partnerships with the estate of Dr. Martin Luther King Jr., as well as alignments with Malcolm X's family. This creation of multicultural learning through cards, posters, and curricula featuring prominent African-Americans, Hispanic-Americans, American Indians, and American women included distribution in schools, through the Smithsonian Institution, and the US Post Office.

He now volunteers at Greenwich Hospital in outpatient oncology and works with several nonprofit groups, lending his helping hands where he can.

ACKNOWLEDGMENTS

I want to thank my son, Michael, CEO of Wicked Cow Studios, for providing me loving perspective and support. His staff was incredible: Frank, Mallory, Matt, and Sam—thank you.

Team Andrews McMeel: Patty, Kirsty, and Tim, thank you for the platform to allow me to share my life's thoughts and insights. You made it fun.

And to my magnificent significant other, Lois, who helped me keep my eye on the ball. And, of course, to Brenda and Lisa: You are so much a part of this, always.

Finally, to you, the reader, I hope you get as much from this book as I got from writing it.

Andrews McMeel Publishing
a division of Andrews McMeel Universal
1130 Walnut Street, Kansas City, Missouri 64106

www.andrewsmcmeel.com

17 18 19 20 21 RLP 10 9 8 7 6 5 4 3 2 1

ISBN: 978-1-4494-8671-6

Library of Congress Control Number: 2017940894

Editor: Patty Rice, Michael Hermann
Creative Director: Tim Lynch, Samantha Merley
Production Editor: Amy Strassner
Production Manager: Tamara Haus

ATTENTION: SCHOOLS AND BUSINESSES

Andrews McMeel books are available at quantity discounts with bulk
purchase for educational, business, or sales promotional use.
For information, please e-mail the Andrews McMeel Publishing
Special Sales Department: specialsales@amuniversal.com.